Hip-Hop!

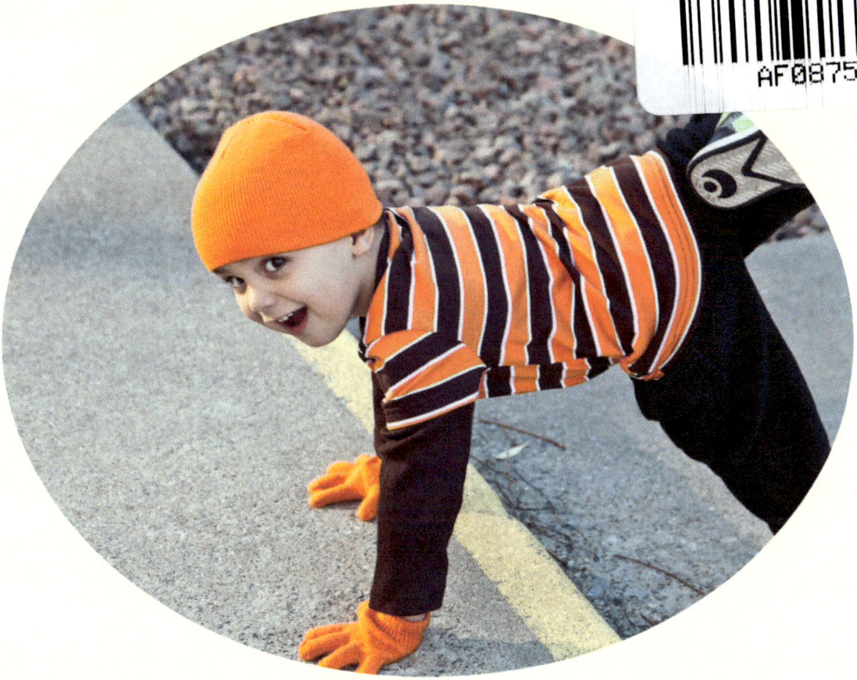

Written by Gill Budgell

RISING STARS

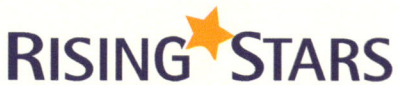

pop

rap

rock

hip-hop

fun

Talk about the book

Ask your child these questions:

1. What type of music are children dancing to at the beginning of the book?

2. How many children are in the rock band?

3. Are the children dancing hip-hop inside or outside?

4. What do you need to rap?

5. What would you play or do in a band?

6. What is your favourite type of music?